Quiet Money

Quiet Money

Poems

Robert McDowell

Story Line Press | *Pasadena, CA*

Layout by Eleanor Goodrich

ISBN 978-1-58654-056-2 (softcover)
     978-1-58654-081-4 (casebound)

Acknowledgments: The author wishes to acknowledge and thank the editors of the
following periodicals in whose pages the following poems first appeared:
   The Chowder Review, "The Liberated Bowler"; *The Hudson Review*, "Coed Day at
the Spa," "The Malady Lingers On," "Poppies," "Quiet Money," "Working a #30 Sash
Tool, Thinking About the Pope"; *Kayak*, "Ballad of Maritime Mike"; *New Jersey Poet-
ry Journal*, "The Cop from Traffic Accident Control"; *Poetry Northwest*, "The Librari-
an After Hours"; and *Washington Review*, "Into the Movies."
   "The Disconnected Party" and "Into a Cordless Phone" are for Mark Jarman;
"Working a #30 Sash Tool, Thinking About the Pope" is for Tom Wilhelmus; "How
Does It Look to You" is for Liam Rector; "Poppies" is for Patricia Aakhus; "Quiet
Money" is for Randy & Carole McDowell; "Into the Movies" is for Michael Aakhus;
"In the Photograph You See" is for Lysa McDowell & Ireland.
   The author wishes to thank especially Robert Cowley. The author is also grateful
to Red Hen Press for reissuing this book.

The National Endowment for the Arts, the Los Angeles County Arts Commission, the
Ahmanson Foundation, the Dwight Stuart Youth Fund, the Max Factor Family Foun-
dation, the Pasadena Tournament of Roses Foundation, the Pasadena Arts & Culture
Commission and the City of Pasadena Cultural Affairs Division, the City of Los An-
geles Department of Cultural Affairs, the Audrey & Sydney Irmas Charitable Founda-
tion, the Kinder Morgan Foundation, the Allergan Foundation, the Meta and George
Rosenberg Foundation, and the Riordan Foundation partially support Red Hen Press.

Second Edition
Published by Story Line Press
an imprint of Red Hen Press
www.redhen.org

for Frederick Morgan, George Hitchcock,
& for Lysa

"It is the word of life," the parent cried;
—"This is the life itself," the boy replied.
                                        —George Crabbe

Contents

1

2

3

1

The Disconnected Party

I lean into my cell, planning a call
To someone I have missed for twenty years.
I look out at the threatening neighborhood
And wonder how I ever grew up here.
I watch three teens on bikes come up the street,
Slow down, and slap my window while passing by.
I turn in time to meet their bully smiles
With a street-tough look I worked on hard in mirrors.
Convincing, I guess, because they do not stop
To pull me from my car. I focus on
The call again and stop. What do I want?
What can Hansen say to justify
The breaking of our friendship years ago?
He wandered off that night with a cordless phone,
And though I called I never brought him back.

You could say Angry was the way I felt.
After all, I was up all night
Dialing his number. I phoned Emergency,
His wife . . . I even got the cops involved.
The next day I was edgy at the job
And told my boss to shove it when he choked
On figures I had put before the Board.
After the meeting, he told me—you can guess.
He clasped his hands together on his desk
(the knuckles white, and each hand looking as if
it didn't like the other) and said to me

"Clean out your desk. Your tenure here is up."

He said a lot of other muscle things,
But I was looking down, tuning out.
I had my hand around a paperweight,
The fifty-dollar kind from some boutique.
Somewhere between *incompetent* and *ass*

I pitched a wicked hard one at his belt.
His eyes popped out like eyes do in cartoons;
His red cheeks ripened to purple and he seemed
To swallow every sentence he'd spat out.
I yanked the blotter from his desk and laughed;
I slapped his face with his appointment book,
Then bounced his nameplate off a tapestry
He'd paid top dollar for. I wasn't through.
He had a gilded letter opener
He loved to fiddle with. I snatched it up
And rearranged the pattern of his couch.
Dragging him by his tie out on the floor,
I sat on him and yelled *Let's Horseback Ride!*
I thwacked his bottom with his favorite knife.

That's when Security discovered us.
One laid me out with something across my back;
Another bounced a sucker punch off my chin.
When I came to, they had me down, in cuffs,
And soon they tossed me into a black-and-white.
I did some time. I worked. I ate. I slept.
When I got out I followed 80 east,
Working a shopping list of stupid jobs.
Now I guess I'm where I meant to be—
Eight digits away from finishing that talk
That got me sidetracked twenty years ago.

    The ringing stopped. Electrocution music
Jolted him, and a familiar tune
From old-time radio made him quiver.
I know this, he was thinking, as the music
Faded under echoing, urgent voices.
And then he awoke: *I Love a Mystery*

Was greeting him instead of his oldest friend.
Jack and Doc fought He-bats on a ledge,
The program's signature gong was pounding, then
A voice said *Leave Your Message at the Beep.*
Was that his friend? A stranger with his name?
Instead of stating simply who he was,
He laughed low like The Shadow and hung up.
I'll greet him where he lives, he told himself.

   His former buddy lived in the same place,
A ranch house in a safe suburban tract.
The neighborhood was working. He checked the street
From the side porch and jimmied back the door.
Inside, he bumped his hip against a dryer
And slid his fingers up the wall for light.
He saw a paper spread across the table
In the breakfast nook, and one dish
Stained with egg looked up at him. He sat.
Picking his way through news he thought of change.
He muttered into the emptiness of House
And thought of opening drawers, changing clothes,
Leaving his dirty shirt out on the bed.
Instead, he found a beer behind some milk
And feeling like an owner made a tour.

The living room was built around TV,
Its carpet a drab and filthy, sullen shag
Of many shifty colors. Stepping over
People magazine and peanut butter
Squares, he tapped the daughter's plywood door
And found a room of boxes. Of course. She's grown,
He said to himself reflected in packing tape.
He rushed the master bedroom down the hall.
As he remembered it the room was dark.

The bed was old, settling into itself.
Was it the one they'd sat on, drinking beer
The last time he'd been here? He tried it out,
And lying down the jokes came back to him,
Setups and their punch lines as good as new.
He laughed. The bottle jiggled on his belly.
That was funny twenty years ago,
But this is now. What am I laughing at?
What little light came in was snuffed by clouds,
And in that dark room from another life
He put the easy, laughing past aside.

He hunted in every room for a cordless phone.
He found two chargers, but neither had their cells.
A sore lump was rising in his throat,
And sweat was backing up between his toes.
Whose house is this? he pleaded, looking up.
And then he saw a door he'd overlooked,
Just off the washroom behind an ironing board.
It all came back—the nights in Hansen's man cave,
Smoking cigarettes and drinking beer
Until they slurred their sentences and slept.

On the arm of a giant chair he found a cell,
And as he gripped it hard he felt alone
Again, abandoned on its frequency.
He thought of surfers caught in the curl of a wave,
A glider pilot losing altitude,
A child waking in a strange bedroom.
He thought *this feeling never goes away*
No matter what you force yourself to do.
Since birth I've misplaced faces, lost myself,
And never known how to call them back.

He staggered on the stairs when a bell went off,
Then took them three at a time to the kitchen phone.
No need to rush, the prerecorded message
Took over as he leaned against the sink.
He turned and worked the answering machine.
He said to it *Guess Who? This Is Your Life*,
Then laughed his Shadow-laugh. Pocketing
The mysterious cell he stepped out on the porch.
The large backyard was dark and overgrown.
He entered it. He kept on walking. Home.

The Librarian After Hours

She has it by heart, the mechanics of his trap,
A blood moon promising luck.
Settling onto the porch with a glass of Glen Ellen '81
She has what she needs to travel—
Good weather inside her,
True-life tales committed to memory,
Her summer guests gone home to their autumn faces.

Now she is hunting beside the pioneer
Who lived so long on opossum
He ate everything raw.
"One appetite spawns another," she says,
Nodding her head at the turn of each page
Until she wanders back, mulling over
Certain meals at which despair sat down
And seemed to crop the centerpiece.
Conversation rubbed too much skin away.
"Nobody leaves the table satisfied," she says.
Her book rides the current in her lap

And the architect comes back, picking at crepes.
"That hospital was earthquake-proof," he said,
But there were seventy people dead.
His wife, the ceramist, squeezed bread as he spoke
And shut him out with strident talk of pots
That held whatever they were meant to.
"Stop fussing with your food," she said,
Speaking too loud to spare him.

"Do you wonder what you're eating?" the hostess asked.
Not unlike the meal she served the beekeeper
Who checked a hive under the eaves and later proposed.
She made him speak of himself.
Unbuttoned by brandy and cigars

He rambled on about his lonely life among bees.
Noting how he glanced repeatedly at the phone
She sent him staggering to his car
While she rejoined her opossum-devouring pioneer.

Suddenly the midnight opossum appears,
Plodding through ivy to empty her coop of eggs.
The librarian's tidy appearance sags
As she closes her book and leans over it.
"There is no hunger like your look," she whispers.
When the trapdoor clacks she rises;
In the coop she corners her fattest red.
As she squats beside it, awash in porchlight,
The ivy-trellised cage rocks and ceases.
The red is a chaos of feathers;
Soon the opossum will twitch in a roasting pan.
If tomorrow the beekeeper calls at work,
If high school students cut up in the stacks,
She will stamp them with gentle reminders,
Then maybe invite them home for a meal.
She sees them clearly as she cooks all night—
The beekeeper retreats into reference books,
The students open their journals and disappear.

Then she punches the ticket out of herself
And pulls back the flap of a covered wagon.
She scans the nothing the future will call her land
For a glimpse of a trapper shouldering dinner.
She waits with a pot and wooden spoon
For mouths to feed, appetites to satisfy,
And says
            "I serve as an outpost, a sponge to hunger,
A scrapbook of obscure survival tips.
I am the chair with an ear,

The cook and comforter on desolation's porch.
Relax to the scratching of knives and forks,
Sweating pitchers of lemon water.
Believe that your confessions are worthy of books,
That no matter the names of courses
You are eating a marvelous story."

The Cop from Traffic Accident Control

The driver's knees went soft as warm butter.
Minute beads of sweat on his forehead
Gave the lie to the concrete look on his face
As he put one slug behind my buddy's ear.
I don't remember much about getting the call.
I believe I thought of the polar ice cap,
Of the possibility that I was having
An out-of-the-body experience.

Out of the body or not I arrived
And ran down the shooter in an alley.
The official report confirms he tripped
And my left front tire crushed his skull.
I believe I thought of my mother when he screamed,
Which didn't help. Then I just froze behind the wheel,
Exhausted, counting garbage cans up ahead.
I still remember the throbbing beet-red stump.

During my suspension I had time
To play back every illusion I'd swallowed whole—
How I dreamed of squad cars sweet as magnolias
Gliding down to comfort city streets,
Cells for the truly needy, keeping the cold out,
And nightsticks no worse than a father's love-tap.
At sixteen, hurling a javelin into the sun,
I never imagined the look I'm wearing now.

Some nights I dream I hide myself in the park,
Coming among the lovers like a cold rain.
Arriving late, pulling them from the wreckage,
Sometimes I dream I hear their loved ones weeping.
And what they say of me is true:
That I arrive, a spit-and-polish mop-up,
Reinstated, man with a cancelled expression
And a flat-top haircut, out of date.

Working a #30 Sash Tool, Thinking About the Pope

"There is no hurt in my profession," Buck muttered,
Checking a door for skippers.
He felt ravenous for spaghetti
And glanced at his watch—10:30.
"I'm tough," he mumbled, "I can take it."
He worked like that awhile, taunted
By the vision of a savory meat sauce.

Meanwhile the radio updated the Pope's condition.
His Holiness was dead, was gravely wounded.
The Pope escaped serious injury.
Bystanders were injured or praying.
One bullet was fired and there were many,
The shooter acted alone and with others.

Buck was furious. He hated
The voices feeding him news, and he
Hated the wimps whining for gun control.
He spat out the word *foreigners* and grumbled,
Thinking how they talked funny and caused trouble.

Working, hurting, Buck came up with a program of blood control.
He wondered exactly how his country might do that
And did not think of his Scotch and German ancestors.
He was American, the best damn painter in Los Angeles.
Didn't he mix his own colors?
Hadn't he won the unofficial contest?

"Nobody will shoot me in this line," Buck stammered,
Then he crossed himself and prayed for the Pope.
Twenty feet up on the ladder he felt close to God and thought
Of the Pope falling into the arms of his secretary.
Had he fallen like a lovesick girl,
Or like a child walking a ledge,
Astonished at missing a step?

These soft images were strange, even foreign.
Flustered, Buck shook himself thinking,
"He fell like any man shot in a jeep."
But an inside voice kept saying
                              The Pope is not a man.
Buck finished off a run of putty
And spoke as wood might speak—
                              "He fell."

To calm himself, Buck thought about his wife,
Happy in her kitchen, who had probably
Turned the radio off, hating the terror
And intrusion on her easy listening.
He imagined her greeting him in the driveway,
A woman priding herself on never making
Unpleasant connections. He'd puff up like bread
In her arms and she'd say something like
                                   "Isn't it awful?
Guess what we're having for dinner?"

    "The world is sick but I'm getting by," Buck snarled,
Working a toothbrush dipped in thinner under his nails.

He was looking ahead to the Lodge
And a round of golf,
To the next job and the next.
He was doing his part, the things he knew,
Not for himself, his wife, or The Pope,
Not for you or me. Just doing it.

Coed Day at the Spa

Sunday. He ought to be in church,
But he's here instead to sweat with women.
Bicycle wheels hum, treadmills grind
Like equations in a teacher's faulty lesson plan.
One smart-ass reads a novel on his bike;
Another, humping language, gulps air
Between each word about the local news—
The fortunes of the AAA ball team,
Who shot the mayor, the widening of Division Street.
Then Reverend Bill swoops in with glad hands,
Yakking it up for God.

Only women are working like they mean it,
Their burrowing expressions screwed on tight as lug nuts.
They do not pause between stations.
They do not loiter round the fountain
Taking in the sights. They do not care
How much your jumpsuit cost or what you do for pay.
Kisses, wine and candlelight
Result in cellulite and loathsome flab.
They fight it, breaking themselves on incline boards,
Shrieking like whistles blown in a closet.
They rise like Lazarus and spread the word.

He stretches in a corner, shy and misunderstood.
He knows The Women group him with the others,
One more Jupiter with microscopic prick
Who lifts to show his strength—
One big push and he's done.
He opposes this with many repetitions,
Ending flat on his back, wheezing like a bellows.
"You ought to give up smoking," Ms. Tri-State says.
"Do you always shave before a workout?"
"Do you?" he counters. She smiles like a spasm.
"Let's pump some iron," she says.

So it's him she wants. She knows
The subtle art of shrinking men.
On the curl machine she is tireless,
On the bench press she cranks out twenty reps at 225.
Nobody presses like her, least of all himself.
Though he's added half a size to his neck,
Though his arms, once thin and flaky
As chicken legs in a Crock pot, bulge with terror,
He lies down like a victim, overmatched.
Looking up he asks, "Do you think this might be love?"
She sets the weight. Laughter swells like a bicep.

The Malady Lingers On

Bill Davis. The name a clairvoyant
Spelled in the palm of her hand.
Tina makes like it's no big deal,
But she's willing, even desperate,
To meet the man the seer describes.
That is enough to bring her to Madame Faye.
That and a carload of friends needing breaks
From husbands who never call them *princess* anymore.

Tina's story began on a farm
In southern Illinois in the 1950s.
She fears that it stops there, too.
At age 5, turning cartwheels on her bed,
She crashed through a window.
The damage to herself was minor
And her mother wept. Daddy paddled her behind.
Come Sunday the family knelt in church.

She was guilty. She knew it.
She was guilty undressing dolls in her sister's bedroom,
Guilty as a cheerleader at 16.
That was tough competition for prayer—
Human pyramids and athletes sassy in their sweats.

But she was not long satisfied with kids her age.
She was after something else
And found it with a local boy just out of the Marines.
Sleek as a halfback, the boy was all God and Country.
When he said, in so many words, that he *was* a god
She said *why not* and let him in.
In no time at all the mother of many children
And living in the suburbs (and not yet 22) she said,
"it felt like the beginning of a story."

Bill Davis, home from work, uncaps a beer
And reads *The Wall Street Journal*. The economy
Is bad and he feels it in his gut.
He replays the day's events, his public self.
"Nobody knows my true worth," he muses,
"Least of all myself." He says,
"The only thing worse than breaking down
In public is breaking down when you're alone."
The thought clasps him until well after sunset.

"You don't know what a help you are," he says to Cat.
"Evenings when I cannot tell the house
From all the others on the block
I look for you in the window.
Are you looking for me? I wish you'd speak."

Night after night he watches the news with Cat,
Which is to say alone, or reads a book,
Or works his thumbs and ponders what he was—
A kid who one day thought he'd spruce the fish pond up
By pouring antiseptics in it.
Nobody said a word but he was proud
Until the fish surfaced, belly-up and bloated.

Tina says to her friends, "Let's grab a drink."
Inside the bar she heads for the Ladies' Room
Where she looks up Davis in the phone book.
"Hundreds," she hisses, "and a dozen Williams."
She clasps her handbag shut as if slamming a door
And stalks out to a margarita.

Meanwhile, Bill is bored with books and TV.
If a stranger called and said his name came up
In her hand that afternoon would he believe it?
He suffers from indigestion and rubs his face,
Thinking he needs a shave. He thinks of Cat,
But he will not shave for her.
He wonders if he should sit in her lap.
"Maybe I should just tie her up," he mutters,
and wonders if *he* would like to be tied up.
He thinks of his escape trumpeted on the news.
His chest swells.

Tina bites her lower lip
And stamps out her cigarette.
"Butt-end of another boring day," she says,
Then weaves out through the parking lot.

After several struggling minutes Bill is ready—
Hog-tied he kneels on a kitchen chair,
A noose around his neck,
The rope knotted round a water pipe.
Sockless, red in the face, he tries
To free his hands. The chair rocks.

Maybe a neighbor glancing through a window
Will spot him and call the cops.
Or Tina may arrive, checking addresses
From the page she ripped out of the phone book.
Bill and Tina will turn up eventually,
But in what condition?
Neither one is thrilled about tonight.

How Does It Look to You

Listen, friend, I saw him use a Bic
To light his pipe. We'd just climbed into the car,
I looked over and poof! He'd lost his face.
That damn thing going off in a closed car
Took me back to popguns we'd packed in school,
But there he was, thirty, burning up!
We'd warned him, too, to chuck that flamethrower,
But he'd crank it up as high as it would go
And laugh at smokers jerking back their heads.
I grabbed it from him once and turned it down,
But in his hands again he wound it up.
Why? *Protection*, he would say sometimes,
Sometimes *It's a conversation starter*.
Every now and then he'd say real low
How he hated folks with bedroom lashes.
He had them, too! But now he needn't worry.

I hit-and-ran red lights to Emergency
Then drove for his wife who screamed when we rushed in.
After the scream, she ran. In high heels yet!
It took me a city block to reach for her,
And when I did she took a swing at me
With her purse, raising a grape on the tip of my ear.
The purse went down, and every item in it
Scattered across concrete. I had her wrists,
Then two men dropped a dolly and had me.
My arms were tied like pretzels up my back,
And something hard and heavy pressed my neck.
One guy hissed *I got him. Get police!*
I saw some shoes run off. I tried to speak.
But all I could make was a little croaking sound.
From where I lay I couldn't see high heels
But I could hear her screaming *Watch His Face!*
My mind was fuzzy by the time I heard

A squad car stop. The handcuffs bit but good,
Strong hands rolled me over, sat me up,
And sun-glare off a badge blinded me.
A voice said *After the lady's purse, creep?*
I caught my wind, laughing long and loud.
My shoulder caught a jab from a nightstick
And that shrill voice was screaming *Not His Face!*

When I could talk again I didn't laugh,
Remembering how I'd seen a joke blow up.
I stared at knees, explained the accident,
The way the victim's wife had run away
And what she'd done to me. They stood me up.
One cop behind me took away his charms
And six of us marched back to Emergency.
My friend was gone, transferred to a Burn Center,
And I thought about how much he'd laugh at me.
A doctor seconded my story.
                                        I was free.

The Workboot Boys went back to their Loading Zone;
The cops took off after making apologies.
The woman got a hypo, pawed at her nose,
And even after I thought she'd gone to sleep
Made disturbing gestures toward her face—
Like someone drowsing, waving off mosquitoes.
She muttered, too. The only words I caught
Were *No* and *Face.* Not strung together, mind,
But free-floating, striking her like bites or stings.

    Outside, the sun was hot. The gutter stunk.
My earlobe tingled—antiseptic wash—
My shoulder ached. I hunted up a drink
And thought of my pal and his wife.

He'd recover, work for an agency,
And do ok with low visibility.
She might learn to look at him and smile;
She might just leave a note and walk away.
I wondered what she'd dream about that night,
But I had my face to feel and think about.
I sat there drinking until the bar closed down,
Then walked on home and put my face to bed.

I counted matches striking one by one
And finally dozed around three. I wish I hadn't.
I felt her high heels stab my back and legs,
And she was chanting words I couldn't reach.
Then a pastor rolled me over, waving his hand
Above my face, and I was lifted up.
He placed her hand in mine, recited verse,
And married us right there in a Loading Zone!
We stood together, learning with every stroke
Our lips, chins, noses, cheeks, foreheads, hair.
A scar-faced crowd pressed all around us, moaning.
We shut our eyes.
                    She whispered *Honeymoon*
And we were checked in to a House of Mirrors.
In every room we entered we were new.
One morning we were three feet tall and fat;
At lunch, we looked like giants with long bones;
At dinner, we admired our shoulder wings.
She said *Next week we'll open the Animal Rooms*.
Who knows how long we lived there? Long enough
To learn to love variety in looks.
Distortion is the gift of second sight.
Did I say that? Did she?

Today I visited my trickster friend.
I got close to the bandages and talked.

He lay there like a matchbook on a street
But faintly squeezed my hand as I got up.
I knew just what that meant and called his wife.
We talked an hour. I asked her out to lunch.
Imagine where I'll take her after that.

Poppies

I can't find a book to help me out of where I am.
I remember the day we drove out to the fields,
Or rather the day I drove out with our friends.
You had to work, but you were with us just the same.
It was still an age of pet names and horizons.
I had been reading "The Mysterious Stranger" by Mark Twain
And I climbed each hill hoping to meet him.
Nothing could have been stranger—
The California desert a-dazzle with poppies.

Drinking beer, we thought of the Land of Oz,
Of lions, tin and straw.
Though we felt a little ashamed for thinking of them
(We were not in school any longer),
Though we were fond of reminding ourselves of what was real,
We didn't fight it when on a nearby hill we saw
A girl like you dancing in her ruby slippers.
Late in the day we split up and I climbed
Until voices called me back. Running

I was Alice pursuing the white rabbit.
When I put my foot in a hole and tumbled down
I was Jack with an empty pail of water.
Waiting for the pain to let up I imagined
Around the World in 80 Days,
My ankle soaring as crowds cheered.
Oh yes there were moments of delight,
Stories I felt a sure part of,
Days in which you and I were perfect.

Into a Cordless Phone

On Reelection Night the news was bad.
He called his oldest friend. They talked for hours,
Cursing groundhogs chewing up the line,
Transcontinental gobblers. His friend was trying
Out a cordless phone.
                                        "I'm moving now,"
He said, pushing through the back screen door.

"I cut my grass early this afternoon.
It looks just like the flattop cut you wore
In school. Suzy loved to skate her palm
Across your varsity plateau until
You graduated to the shaggy look.
I'm not the one who got invited to
Her parents' cabin at Lake Arrowhead!
Her family OK'd only right-wing nerds
Like Eddie Planck and Nehemiah Boone.
So tell me who you voted for. You won't?
Go walk along an unemployment line
And see how they take the news. You've done it? Where!"

He didn't catch the response of the unemployed
Because the corded voice had broken up.
I have no line, he thought, and glanced at stars
As if an operator might appear.
Instead a shooting star arced east to west
And something to his inner ear said *Walk*.
So heading west he crossed his neighbor's yard.
He stopped to stroke a basset hound, then dialed
His cordless phone and said hello. A sound
Washed over static, buried it in verbs—
"Run! Pack! Get your things and go!"
The dog he was scratching yelped and shook its head.
The crash of something falling shot from the house.
"Hello!" he said to the phone. "Hello! Hello!"
A wave of static rolled in to answer him.

He hurried past the house and crossed the street
To Earhart Park. By the lake the phone was silent.
Only laughter from a grove off to his right
Came in to him. He heard a bottle break
And hurried on until he faced her statue.
Staring up at the missing aviatrix
He raised his phone and spoke. "Come in," he said,
"For God's sake tell me where you are tonight."
The statue stared as if he didn't exist,
And nothing on his phone disputed it.
Farther down the path he chose a spot
To lean against a pole and warm his face
In yellow light that made the stars go out.
He thought of spy planes grazing the bleak Pacific;
He thought of rumors never verified
And wandered into the Children's Area
Where he sat on a swing and dialed his boyhood home.
Was it his mother he was speaking to?
He talked and talked about a day in school,
Then caught himself, fearing local news:

MAN ON SWING CALLS HOME ON CORDLESS PHONE

His cordless phone was dead, his mother, too.
Amelia hadn't answered. No one spoke.

He left the park and crossed Elm Avenue,
Then circled round the Billings' swimming pool.
Maybe water cleared its frequency,
Because his phone was rafting one low voice:
"You can't sit out there every night," it said.
"Nothing you can do will bring him back."
Another voice was sobbing while it spoke,
As soft as water lapping in the pool.
Then crying leveled off in a woman's voice

"I just ran in to get the phone," she said.
"He was sitting in his playpen in the sun."
Her voice collapsed as he pushed through a gate.

The smell of garbage billowed out of cans.
His phone was mad with voices changing every
Twenty steps or so: *Sausage and anchovies—*
Feed the dog or shoot it! I don't care!—
I told you never play with Daddy's eyes!—
Take this, please, and try to get some sleep.—

He thought he should hang up but couldn't bring
Himself to disconnect his neighborhood.
He ducked a squad car, ducking behind a hedge,
And tried to eavesdrop on their radio.
He dialed 911 and said *Police*;
Another voice screamed *Fire* and he ran.
Crossing a familiar lawn he hopped a fence,
Then crept up to a door and dialed his phone.
"Hello," he whispered, "can you hear me now?"
His daughter's southern drawl was sweet with sleep.
"Go call your mother to the phone," he said.
His wife came on. She said his voice was odd,
"Like someone's sitting in a well," she said.
His friend's long-distance, earnest voice broke in
But faded after shouting the word *Where*.
He said to his wife "I will not sleep tonight,"
But he dropped the phone on the lawn and went inside.

2

Quiet Money

The bootlegger opens his eyes and stares
Down the gray runway, another Wednesday.
Bony, shivering in early bathroom weather,
He gropes for a glass of rye on the windowsill
And flicks on the light. Flight day.
The weather report on the wireless is good,
Though what he sees in his shaving mirror
Makes him think of mechanical foul-ups—
A slice of wing shooting past him,
Propeller chips smacking against his goggles.

Flicking his thumb across a straight razor,
Joe tells himself it's good to feel the edge,
To remember it's only a membrane or a veil
That separates blood from the body intact.
He thinks of blood, the body breaking apart.
He imagines a membrane holding it all in.
He thinks of landing an office job and laughs,
Thinks of coffee in a field cup and he's warm.
Two alley cats howl, toppling a trash can.
"That's motivating music," he says,
And mutters the closing bars of *Over There*—

Betty sulks in a luncheonette on Fourth.
Daubing her nose with a hankie, stirring eggs,
She wants him. She wants him everywhere.
On the bus to work she thought of telling him,
"Give it up or stop coming around,"
But the words were too heavy to carry,
Like too much weight in her handbag
Throwing off her natural stride.

Now she laughs
At the thing she'd tried last night,
Pouring so many martinis, hoping he'd nosedive

Into a bottomless sleep and miss this day.
But Joe can hold his liquor, especially when
He's talking poetry and war. Later,
Betty can't remember the hour she passed out,
Or the minute he pinned the note to her pillow.

> *See you Monday, Doll Face,*
> *With something pretty from Paris.*

The airstrip flags point east at a quarter to five.
Joe rubs the compass in his flight jacket pocket,
His fingers brushing the pages of Wilfred Owen,
And he's thinking of wings.
Not those of machines, but of birds,
What he'd wanted as a child
Who had loved the bird's life of recklessness
And dramatic death down a chimney
Or in the talons of a larger bird.
Walking around the plane he whistles.

"Nobody knows," he mutters, "but some Frenchmen miles away.
'Nobody crosses The Pond alone,' the experts say.
Well, I won't be rubbing their noses in it,
Though there's plenty gearing up to do just that.
Circus flyboy stuff. There's money in it,
But fame comes with it, too—a suit you can't take off."

He lingers, checking the Wright Whirlwind engine.
The headwind says *look out*;
His patience says *take off*."
Far to the north the lights of Jersey sparkle,
Calming down.

He scrambles up on the wing, his perch,
One step from home. The cockpit
Makes him think of the backyards of boyhood.
Clearing the stand of trees at the field's far edge,
Joe banks to the left, circling the field,
And levels out heading northeast.
He likes that initial turn, getting the feel of it,
Feeling the earthbound tug slip away.

He imagines gunning for stars,
But the stars are at peace, in collusion.
The sun balloons above the waterline,
The moon drops down to the sea.
Joe thinks of the money he's flying,
Of crates of cognac stacked in a French hanger.
He thinks of a present for Betty, of the life
He's making, up here, among prosperous currents.
-+-
She doesn't want to think of him all day,
But superstition bites. She takes off,
Daydreaming herself into flight beside him.
"Joe," she murmurs, "all I want is a home
With you on the sofa, drinking a soda."
After five, plodding home, her head
Keeps lifting to a drone that isn't there.
"Monday's not far off," she whispers.
-+-
Joe's gruff Parisian contact waves
As he lifts off, climbing in the wind
That will take him back to the luncheonette.
He climbs on the current and the current inside him,
The energy Betty loves him for and fears.

Twelve hours out, twenty from home,
He fights it,

The drone of the motor stirring sleep.
He regrets staying up so late the night before
Singing war songs, talking baseball
And British poets, and women—always women.
Joe nods over the controls,
But something besides sleep isn't right.
Something in the sky is wrong.

He snaps to attention, focusing
On a silver image before him, skimming the sea.
Bird, then *dolphin* occurs to him. Then *plane*.
That can't be, so he tells himself *reflection*
And conjures the creature from an old story
That snatches plane and pilot
If they fly too close to the sea.
"That can't be anyone but me," he says.
The image below him fades, heading the other way.
Joe's relieved, but that's wrong. He cups his hand
Outside to catch a breeze, to deflect it into his face,
But sleep blows through him, too.

Now he's groping for the brainstorm gadget he'd installed
Beneath his seat. He finds it, brushes against the live wire
With his wrist, and sits up, back to himself.
He's alone—as it should be.
Below him nothing angles but the sea.
Hitting fog, he pulls back on the throttle
(Like flying inside a glass of milk)
until he finds clear air at 4,500 feet.
He thinks of Betty asleep,
And of Brown and Alcock
Teaming up to cross the Atlantic first in 1919.
He thinks of them losing their bearings in fog,
Flying upside down within 500 feet of the sea.
How many times did Brown crawl out on the wing,

Wiping snow and sleet from the fuel gauge? Joe smiles.
"Those fellas made good, alright, but what for?
10,000 pounds, knighthood,
And Alcock dead in a crack-up six months later."

Good night, Irene, good night...

Joe tips his wing to Alcock
And levels out over the coast of Newfoundland.
✢
Sweeping cups from the counter into a tray,
Madge winks as Joe saunters past the register.
Betty, raising a fork, freezes,
Riding out a tremor, and a wedge
Of lemon meringue free-falls to her lap.
"You can't wear your food with this," he says.
One hand rests on her shoulder,
The other sets a hatbox on the table.
Tapping the left side of his jacket
He lowers his voice. "Tonight," he says,
"I'll show you what I've got in here."
Betty's face is like clearing weather
As she preens herself in the mirror,
Admires the way she looks in a smart Parisian bonnet.
"Maybe that hat will help you see things differently,"
Joe says. Betty sits down while Joe fidgets with a cup.
"You don't look well," she says. "What's up?"

   "I pushed it to the limit on this run.
I let myself stay up all hours,
And then I couldn't hold it off—
The Sandbag Eye—I saw things.
I saw the creature from that story you hate;
I saw myself as a child, grounded in a strange neighborhood.
I saw another plane, Betty. A reflection, I guess,

But that's what shook me most. Listen,
I got a bonus for the quick turnaround.
It's more than we've ever seen.
Why don't we get hitched?
Just don't ask me to give it all up."

"I know," she says,
And hammers one hard kiss across his chapped lips.

On the street, Joe feels the slap of a newsboy's cry:

Lindbergh Lands in Paris!

Joe whistles like a punctured tire.
Betty, nodding, hugs his arm.
"I didn't want to bring it up," she says.
Joe leans against a lamppost, staring east.

  "Lindbergh.
I never thought he'd beat them,
Byrd and the others with their bankrolls.
I knew he was in the hunt, in a quiet way,
But I never figured this.
He'll get tickertape parades and medals now,
Money and keys to the mayor's w.c.
Think of it, honey, all that brotherly love."

On the landing, at the door to her walk-up,
Betty fumbles in her purse for keys.
"At least Lindbergh's never landed *here*," Joe says.
Inside, he pulls a bottle from his duffel bag.

  "Sometimes a proud man
Doesn't wave himself around," Joe says.
"Headlines cut the pants off privacy.

They make you public, a pioneer.
I wonder if he knows what he's in for?"

Joe talks and talks
As the moon pins a spotlight on his face.
Betty wrings her hands and rocks,
The bottle open on the bureau-top,
But neither takes a drink.

—+—

Past three, Joe is flying blind, questioning.
Betty's breathing is a motor in good repair.
Joe hums under his partner's sleep.
"What?" she murmurs, banking out of a dream.
"I'm thinking of getting a house in Jersey," he says,
But he's thinking of Lindbergh, too.
He's thinking of a plane below him,
Skimming the rooftops of Paris, beating him out.
"Anywhere," Betty says. "Anything you want."

What *does* he want?

Nearing five, Joe looks down at his body in a restless sleep.
Sprawling so, he looks a little like Italy on a globe.
Out of the body, a body looks that way,
A smear of papier-maché, a flare-up,
An ugly reminder on a fist of blue.
Joe, or Joe's double, wonders
If the quiet atmosphere he flew in was a cheat.
Betty, asleep, looks like a separate country.
How can she make him believe in home?
In peace? Can anyone? Undertakers, maybe—
White-jacketed illusionists keeping a low profile.
Why does Joe's double escape so many nights?
Why, when he returns, does he keep
What he's found to himself,

A country inside a country, unmapped?
The questions hound Joe out of sleep,
So wrapping himself in a blanket,
He gropes his way into a chair
And flicks on the reading lamp.
Slowly the room settles, focuses,
And he picks up a copy of Lear
To whisper the fool's lines, his favorites.
Their sound, the way it makes him feel,
Is enough. He rides it into the afternoon.

On moving day they look like a couple
In a paperweight, their arms around each other.
Joe is Errol Flynn in a flight jacket;
Betty's lucky hair falls down like rain.

After the movers back over the curb
And putter north, the newlyweds
Climb the fire escape for a farewell drink.
"What are you thinking?" she asks.

"Nothing. Just noticing the wind,
How it's turning nasty, how I wouldn't wait."
The winner in the paperweight dissolves;
A hard and lonely figure takes his place.

"Joe, how long before you face it,
Before you get it straight—what it means to you?"
"What are you talking about?"
"Not what," she says. "Who."

Joe faces her. "Don't push," he says,
And suddenly he sees himself as memory,
His image fraying like tapestry.
"I hope you can take it," he says. "Your man's obscurity."

—|—

"Something Willy said just ticked Joe off,"
Betty tells her neighbor in the backyard.
The iron fence between them soaks up heat.
"I don't know what."

"I do," her neighbor says. "Willy was carrying on
About the Yankees and the Babe.
You know how men get hot when talking sports.
Well, Joe claimed that there were players in obscure leagues
Who were just as good as Ruth but never got the breaks.
Willy wasn't buying, and soon they were toe-to-toe.
Their faces got red, the veins in Joe's neck popped out.
I noticed that just before he did it—
Threw his glass (I swear it nicked Willy's ear) in the pool."

"That's when I came out," Betty says.
"I saw Willy's eyes get big like balloons
And Joe just turning, walking away.
He passed right by me and didn't speak,
Though I could feel anger breathing out of him.
It goes back further than the Yanks and the Babe."

A drone out of the west breaks in
And both women look up
As Betty's single-engine fly-boy tips his wing.
Anna gurgles in her playpen.
Chug, their terrier, snoozes on a plank of sunlight.
The plane levels off, descending
To the airstrip a couple of miles away.
Betty holds her breath. *Irrational,*
She tells herself, but she can't help it.
Only when he turns their Silver Ghost
Up the drive will the moment be enough,
His coming back in one piece

To lift Anna off his knee,
Catching her as she parachutes back.

—+—

   "I had a case of the yips for years," Joe says.
His nephew, Charley, sips lemonade and nods,
Not knowing what Joe means. He lets him talk.

"After we got hitched,
The weather always indicated stay.
So, I'd scrub a couple of flights a month,
Then two a week, and pretty soon
I was on the ground more hours
Than I was logging in my plane.
Imagine what that did to me!
You never feel the same
Once you've cut through weather
And known it topside. You miss
The motion, the nerve-and-bone collision.

"How many nights did I rock in my chair,
Spending in my head the cash I'd make
As soon as I got home safe? And *safe*—
That word would take me like a haunting
As I'd fall back in this room knowing where I was.
I had it, yes. The Yank dream,
No rain, no sleet, no public pilot
Cutting his silver trail under me,
No flight I couldn't roundtrip in a day.
When I couldn't sleep I'd rock.
I don't know how I put her through
Those shifting moods, but Betty was great.
She'd touch me—stop me, really—
"Level out," she'd murmur,
But if she strayed too long I'd veer off course again,
My throttle hand squeezing nothing,
Making fingernail imprints on its palm.

"I had to face it,
 The need for something to run up against,
 A glass door, a garage wall, a chirping neighbor,
 An impassive, staring hero on the front page.
 Anna helped, and the dog, and this place,
 But I needed more. I got it, too.
 It's sad to think of it now."

At sixteen, Charley perks up to the promise
Of a sad story. He refills his glass,
And without asking does the same for Joe.

"You're a little young to recall firsthand
 the scene I'm thinking of.
 It was March of '32.
 The Lindberghs had a house not far from here
 Outside of Hopewell—ironic name!
 The papers served up their grief like daily bread.
 We memorized photos of ladders
 And footprints in the mud,
 A ransom note on the windowsill.
 The baby, as near as we could tell,
 Was stuffed, still sleeping, in a burlap bag.
 'It looks like the work of pros,' the cops said,
 Which was good for the kid's sake.

"And then the waiting. Ten weeks of dying,
 Ten weeks of cranks and comforters,
 Wheels (the cops called the crazies *wheels*) and volunteers.
 I flew some for the cops, you know,
 Shooting down false leads. It made me sick
 Each time I landed with nothing to offer Lindbergh
 But a negative shake of my head.
 I'll never get the look on his face out of my head.
 It was a mid-Atlantic look, your plane out of fuel.

The clocks ground on but didn't move.
Mail flowed into their house like lava,
And all for nothing. Cruelty.
The body turned up in the woods
A few miles away—and this is the awful part—
He'd been dead since that first night.
The ladder-man dropped the burlap sack,
And the baby's head struck a window ledge.
Imagine how the 'nappers must have felt!

"And Lindbergh. How far out,
   in after-years, did he push himself to feel secure?
And the rest of us . . . how many couldn't sleep
For fear of waking without sons or daughters?
We learned to love the sounds of words
That covered us—words like *lock* and *alarm*,
And we raised you on them.
Now you can't look strangers in the eye,
And there may be secrets
You can't even share with your closest friend.

"Son, you have to lose to win.
That notion settled in us
And we passed it on to you.
Thank God. You know what it meant to me?
My daughter safe, first of all,
And all of it, really.
I spent so many nights in her room
Just watching her sleep,
Convincing myself no gang would take her
From me—ex-fly-boy, average businessman—
And suddenly I was happy.
My life's course felt fair.
I thought of fame and money, and still do,
How what we do to get them can make us sorry.

3

The Backward Strut

When his telephone rings at 3 a.m.
And nobody hangs up and nobody speaks,
It comes to him that childhood
Is so remote it belongs to someone else.
Later, dozing in his favorite chair,
He dreams he can leap into moonlight
And be only vaguely aware
Of children, rebuked, taunting parents,
Of the alley crunching and gobbling, claiming its own.

Awake he sits at table and stares at the phone,
Hoping she'll unlock her language box.
He wonders what the dog knows, lying in a heap,
And the cat whose drug is an open window.
Maybe they'd like to listen to the radio,
But there's too much heartache on the air.
He feels like a man who opens a closet
To find another's clothes hanging inside.

Is he destined to live out his life
A lowercase letter among capitals?
Is he the test chemical that never pans out?
He remembers how at his christening he wiggled,
Evading the holy spray of water.
He thinks how there is no song to fit this life,
How the lyric is just like a wishbone—
A rush from the heart, a crack, and that's that.

The Origin of Fear

The Death Month, August, wears a driver out,
But he is almost home, speeding over
A residential street with his windows down.
A woman on a corner screams or laughs,
Her disembodied cackle crashing in.
He turns. He sees a blur of toothy face

And breaks into the sweat of an eight-year-old.
Melting down his hands run off the wheel.
He squirms against an ice chest in the back.
He fixes on the back of his mother's head
And sticking to the seat he thinks it's beautiful.
An hour goes, an hour of gas and heat
And he is moaning now, pleading for his
Angel of the Douglas Fir to take him home.
But no Angel appears. "Mother," he wants to say,
But she is driving to the radio.
There is barely room in the car for parent and child,
Barely room for the ice chest and winter coats
They'll need up north, barely room for breath.
One window, broken, swallows spanking heat.
"Hang on," his mother says. "Hang on
Until we climb out of L.A." To the child
The drive seems longer than a long, long day.
He tries to think of heroes who hang on,
But soon he retches out the broken window.
Empty then he falls back in his seat
And offers up his spirit to the sun.
He thinks he knows Extermination now.

About the time the nausea returns
The Edsel starts up 99, crossing the Grapevine.
There is nothing to see but Death hills, Death sun,
Then, miracle of miracles, Death

In images he cannot stand to look at.
Fascinated, he stares at a giant billboard
Where a woman like his mother, dressed
In black, weeps above an open casket.
A gray man in a grey suit lies inside.
Their two small grieving children flank the box
While a black oak highway trails off behind.
And over a hill, in the upper left-hand corner,
A black-cowled, risen Death's Head smiles.
Now the boy can feel his own death near,
Though a merciful distraction might dismiss it.
Instead, a second billboard offers up
A scene so dark the boy stares hard to see it.
A sickly moon. A stormy hill of tombstones;
A mother-woman stands before a grave.
The boy looks at her back and feels her tears.
The chill he feels keeps growing as they come
Up on a third billboard, a fourth, a fifth,
All images of Grieving After Death.
In one a suited shadow-man walks off
With Death, his children's faces wailing as
The veiled mother-woman holds them back;
In another a white cross dwarfs the highway;
In the last the smiling Death's Head waits for traffic
Like a parent willing children home.

The boy will never sleep the same again,
Feeling kinship with the broken billboard
Boy and girl, agonizing over
How his mother and the billboard lady looked
So much alike, how the father left
The billboard family, too.
                              But that was years ago.
Today, at thirty-two, he's driving home

While the billboard painter pours himself a drink
Down south in a hillside home, warming up
His voice for the evening air of the Coliseum.
╪

The team from *People* magazine, paid
To feel this way, nod and act enthralled.
"Tell us how His word first came to you,"
The writer says. "Tell us how the artist
Turned to God."
                              Their subject squirms and swallows,
Crunching on an ice cube while he thinks.

"You ever drive up north on 99?
Ever see my work before the Commission
Tore it down?"
                              The *People* people stare,
All natives of the East. Their subject shrugs.
"You know I studied art in Hollywood,
Even shared a studio with Pollock.
I was in a gallery on Melrose then
And sold a painting every three or four months.
Much good it did! Jackson hit New York
And made it big but I . . . I was stuck.
It got so I was lucky just to eat
And then I saw the ad in the *L.A. Times*:

CALL FOR ARTISTS: OPEN COMPETITION!

"The State Highway Commission had a plan
To gag the outcry over traffic deaths
By putting up a string of nightmare billboards
Along the most fatal stretch of road in the system.
I heard a thousand artists sent in slides.
A month went by, another week. I sagged

And for the first time in my life I prayed.
Then I was called.
                              I had a week to sketch
A winning series based on traffic death.
The day of the interview my competition
Laid out gory scenes of mangled steel,
Bodies missing arms, legs, eyes—even heads!
His colors were red, autopsy blue-and-white.
Now me, I kept my colors somber—
Blacks and grays—and focused on survivors,
The grieving Left Behind, women and children
Victimized by witnessing. I focused
On their agony and fear and on
Their grinning master, Death. I'd slow cars down
Through paralyzing shock alone! I said
'Suggestion is more awful than the crash'.

"My argument paid off. They hired me.
I had six months, a massive studio,
A vision I believed was worth my skill.
Day and night I sketched and painted Death—
And not Death you might reason out in time.
I sketched and painted Death and then I prayed.
Michelangelo knew what I'm talking about.
My girlfriend didn't. She said she wouldn't come
To the studio anymore—*couldn't* come—
Because she woke up sweating, dreaming of Death.
One day as I was working on a child
It came to me I hadn't heard from her
In more than a week. And that, my friends, was that.
You wonder did it bother me? Not much.
When the Commission toured my studio
I felt as John the Baptist must have felt

To see the waders changing as they came.
I knew then what my life was all about.
My signs went up.
                                I laid my brushes by.
Often, I would drive up north and park
Just close enough to see the Series whole.
Exulting, I observed the drivers flinch,
Their cars slow, swerve, then pick up speed.
Face to face they'd seen what God could do!
Fatalities declined because The End
Was there on giant boards for all to see.

"I had seen. I read the Scriptures and
At night, I took an elocution class.
I perceived that I must master words.
I'd done the visual, which only reached
The few who drove that way. I dropped my friends
And spoke in bars and unemployment lines.
I pestered the press, pressuring for space
And one fine Letter to the Editor
Led to my first call to address a church.

"The pastor introduced me as a painter
Who had given up a lie for Him.
As he pointed to the ceiling I looked up,
Then took the pulpit to correct his gaffe.
Paint was the avenue he took to me;
My failed life was all I had denied.

"That little talk was good. When it was done
The congregation greeted me with a found look.
From there the invitations multiplied,
As did my following, and then my friends
From local business clubs made clear to me

The need for one sane voice to make a church.
I guess you know the TV part of it.
Today so many hide out in their homes!
I have to get to them in God's New Way."
╬
Nearing ten, the tired man up north
Pours three fingers neat and pulls a downstairs
Chair before the color console screen.
Sitting in the dark, his left-hand strokes
The neutral body of remote control
And thinking of that disembodied scream
He sips his drink and presses. The screen glows,
Then hums and focuses like prophecy.
Feeling a little better, he punches through
The major network news, a canceled show
From nervous boyhood, a horror film.
He doesn't feel enough to stay with these
And turns to cable just in time to see
The L.A. Coliseum from the air.

The next shot is a close-up of a man
Whose manner seems to open like a psalm.
The viewer straightens, leaning in to it.
He tries to create distance with a curse,
But turning to other channels he comes back
To that accusing, urgent voice of doom.
The viewer paws at his stomach, feeling sick
And wonders why he just can't go to bed.
He curses the sleep, for him, that lies ahead
And thinks of words he said above a casket,
His hollow mother, rigid, facing him.
He rubs his eyes then drops his hands and stares.
Unbeliever! I know I'll pay for it.
He witnesses, he moans, he fears his bed.

The Liberated Bowler

Never at the Olympics will she wed,
And never in grandmother's dress
(Who could not break 200 for her life).
Never in church will Ethel forfeit her name,
The pews a refuge for losers and bad sports.
She will take her man in Lane 3
Or not at all, the preacher
In a black coat behind a scorer's table.

"At last, a wife who's functional," Bill says.
"Goodbye to rented shoes and stippled balls;
 Goodbye to the miserable misdirection of my life."
 He cannot wait for the ceremony to end,
 For the honeymoon—two weeks of bowling—to commence.
"Starting out in training is good for a marriage," he says.
 In his mind he masters impossible splits,
 The stare, stride and pure release of a champ.

 Meanwhile Ethel's mother weeps.
"America," Ethel murmurs lovingly to Bill.
 Her eyes are moist, and she rubs the ring
 Made out of bits of her lucky turquois ball.
 When both have said *I do* they bowl a game for luck
 While fellow bowlers sing and toss rice.
"I am happy," Ethel says. "Almost like bowling a perfect game."
 The preacher, signing the license, records a strike.

 Six months later Bill has trouble sleeping.
 Her words as they left the alley haunt him
"In a year I'll count on you for back-up.
 A solid 185 will do."
 He had asked what she would do
 If his game dipped below 185,
 And shuddered when she did not laugh.
"Your average can only go up," she'd said.

On their first anniversary Ethel cannot sleep.
She sits at the kitchen table making little mounds
Out of cigarette ash. Bill, a heavy drinker,
Lies on the bed like defeat.
"I kept my patience for the longest time," she mutters,
"But when bowling for the championship he rolled
A gutter-ball in the tenth I lost it."
Her voice is split in two. She cannot pick it up.

Today Bill dabbles in real estate
And Ethel spends most evenings tuning her game.
The marriage that shook Rockport is memory.
"I want a wife who's functional at something *I* do well,"
Bill tells his buddies during Happy Hour.
Ethel shaves the headpin, picking up a split,
And wishes for a man who can take it,
This thing she does so well.

After the Money's Gone

Hector could not help himself
When he thought of kites, meadows, changeable winds.
Like his namesake he could not win.
When he landed a job, it was always the same.
He would stick it out for a week or two
Then begin to miss his morning bus.
His boss would spot him in the park,
Red in the face, chugging over hills.
Hector would wind in his skein of string
Like a terminal patient, the pink slip
Stuffed in his short pocket, and head for home.

His wife was worth half a dozen jobs.
That's how many he lost before she left him.
"Plant yourself," his buddy told him over beer.
"Hug your swatch of earth
Like it's your own skin.
That's what a woman wants in her man."
Hector knew if he went home he'd stay up
Watching reruns of shows he didn't care for.
He thought of going to church,
But the air in church was bad. He knew
If he thought of his wife he'd begin to cry.

His buddy tossed money on the bar, said goodnight.
"What is it women want?" Hector muttered.
He rubbed the stubble on his face
And thought of bad weather robbing the sky of kites.
"I feel dry though I drink and drink," he said.
He thought of words that could change the look on his face.
He thought of balsa wood and paper,
He thought of wind, miles of white string.
To say their names over and over almost made him smile.
He did not touch another drop that night,
And he was on his way to the park before sunrise.

Ballad of Maritime Mike

The continent depressed him,
   His scurrilous crew rolled dice.
He tuned in an old-time radio show
   And scratched the sheet for lice.

His wife was not there with him
   Though they'd married just recently.
She said if she sailed she'd become someone else—
   She said "No one means *that* to me."

He never wanted to change her,
   To make a ship's mate of his wife.
He thought of someone equal in rank,
   Bread to his butter knife.

He thought of someone equal in rank,
   A thought that made him grieve
Realizing that his wife was the kind
   Who'd pack up her lipstick and leave.

She worked in some government racket
   That doled out cheese to the poor;
She spoke of herself as a guardian of mice.
   If he giggled at that she got sore

And needled his sallow complexion,
   His risky investments gone sour.
She told him to beach his seagoing dream
   And focus on corporate power.

He put his hand in an ashtray,
   Sketched a sail on its floor,
Then hurled it through a picture window
   As she bolted the bathroom door.

She brayed abuse from the tub,
    He whined that he needed to sail
As he had in the war after submarines.
    His grip on the doorknob was frail.

His grip on himself was worse,
    Slick as a soapy plate.
When he came home late a note from his wife
    Said "I'm out on a dinner date."

In lipstick, he scrawled that he loved her
    On the medicine cabinet mirror,
Then he shuffled out with his duffle bag
    While mumbling a sailor's prayer.

He put down money on a hulk
    As big as a PT boat,
Appeared out of place in unsavory bars
    Signing crewmen who'd keep it afloat.

The best were committed to ritzy lines
    The worst drank up his liquor.
Through shoals of ale, through a spray of darts,
    He got just what he paid for.

So, all aboard they waited
    For Providence to package a sign
In the shape of a wind from Alcoa or Sears,
    Like heartbreak the harbor was sighing.

The radio show was scratchy.
    The crew cursed, rolling dice.
The captain's ugly life reared up
    And jerked at his collar twice.

Then a spiritless fish pursued him
  With a mouth like his jilted boss.
Its teeth were grainy with dollar signs,
  Its breath was an anthem of loss.

He wanted to hook that fish
  By reciting appropriate Scripture,
But the door to his learning was webby and cramped.
  He'd never been much of a reader.

Foul weather spotted his compass,
  Failure sat down on his charts.
The crew below plotted to slit his throat.
  Disaster flexed in their hearts.

Meanwhile the captain's wife
  Had hired a crack P.I.
To track him down and cuff him home.
  She'd already had a good cry.

That hunter found him, too,
  In his cabin of turtle light.
He told him that he'd been sent for;
  The captain stood up to fight.

In a minute or two they were puffing
  Like fish reeled out of the sea.
When the captain's shoulder popped he groaned
  "Look what you've done to me!"

The drive from the harbor was poignant
  As the captain blubbered and swooned.
The P.I. wiped a yawn from his face.
  He felt good. It wasn't his wound.

The captain's wife was waiting,
  Her skin looked like Singapore.
He rolled down his window and managed *hello*.
  She smiled and he wanted more.

She tucked him in bed with hot brandy,
  And said she was running late.
She said they had much to talk about
  After her dinner date.

Into the Movies

The sidewalk creeper looks ahead to the Pacific,
To the peal of mission bells.
Stepping out of a drainage tunnel
Under Highway 41 he is happy.
Barges will not keep him up all night.
Someone else can claim his lean-to
And lie awake reading the papers he used for warmth.
Walking north against the suction-slap of semis,
He imagines a pal released from jail,
A worker out of luck,
Then cuts west on Covert. He slows down,
Squeezing the tire of a bike chained to a fence.
There is rain in the weather, the sweat of trees,
Some creature panting in an alley.

Now he's getting what he needs at this time each day
As he makes a withdrawal at Donut Bank.
At the counter, huddled over coffee,
He fidgets with the holes in his socks
And thinks of his favorite moviemaker, Preston Sturges.
He tells himself how Sturges knew the scruffy side
Of money, the steep slide from a stool.
Then he wonders if Sturges ever stared
Through the window of a florist shop
While thinking of blue mountains above a patio
And alimony leveling the landscape out.

He thinks of the look his own wife
Found inside her the night she left—
That empty cash register look.
Dunking a glazed donut,
He plays a Sturges film in his head
And Great McGinty recalls his days as governor
While wiping down a South American bar.
"McGinty lost by playing for people

Instead of himself," he says,
And he's thinking of that bicycle.
—✝—
Back on the street he fingers a wire cutter,
Flinches as a black-and-white zooms by.
The chain snaps. A cat growls in a tree.
In a gust of wind the cables overhead
Sway back and forth, methodical as jump ropes.
He hears a child waking up.
Then he is peddling through a fine spray,
Through a chain-gang scene in *Sullivan's Travels*.
What does he try to forget?
Riding the rails to Hollywood in '46?
The nothing good that happened when he got there?
Fleeting jobs? Hammerhead police?
That last week peddling what he knew about stars—
Maps telling where they lived?
The smell of the train yard counterpunches the past

And he brakes beside a blind man
 Holding up the station house
 Beside a dog that looks asleep, or worse.
"How does John Gilbert's house sound to you?" he says.
"I could take you there."
"I'm anywhere," the blind man says,
 and makes his squeeze-box wail,
 which makes the dog's ear twitch,
 which agitates the fly on his brow.
"You can leave the bike," he says.
"It's good to have conveyance.
 Anywhere's OK, but there are places even after that.
 I'd like a private way to get there should I go.
 Maybe I could hook a basket up for dog."
The creeper and the blind man laugh. The 6:05 blows by.

"Only in America," the creeper says, "could Sturges make it;
Laughter in an ambulance, everybody crooked but OK,
Easy marks, loose change, no change.
They say he liked to park his private car
In an alley and sing to himself all night."
He leans the bike against the blind man's leg.
"I'm going to try," he says.
"Now file those numbers off. I'll say
That southern chain-gang scene one more time,
The one with convicts laughing at cartoons."
The creeper did that, crossed four tracks, and hopped the flyer west.

In the Photograph You See

"You rub a woolen trouser leg like this."
He tells me as he pins my cuffs,
All red in the face from bending.
The motion his hand makes on fabric
Is like love,
A silent magic between man and dog.
I copy his motion,
Rubbing self-consciously along one thigh.
"It feels like—wool," I say.

Glancing down at his bald head
I think of children's clowns on American TV.
I think of money and he taps me
Behind a knee saying "Stand up straight!
Don't regret the money!
Hats are in,
Hemlines fall,
And we are easier to look at."

I tell him my legs are different lengths.
"Of course," he says. "I will make one memory shorter."
Is that what wool-rubbing gets me?
"You Yanks are slow to believe," he says.
"Practice some in private. Relax
And go like this."

What do you see?

"I am twenty-three and thin," he says,
"At the shore with my Bride-to-be.
It is August
And it is that hot, too.
The windbreaks down the beach buckle and snap back,
As bright as band uniforms on a saint's day.
The sun sets, a full moon grazes the water—

And there's more I'd rather not say."
He winks.
"Come back this afternoon at three."

    After three I swing the trousers in a sack.
I prize them as I pace the shopper's street.
I praise the trousers, regretting money,
And hop the #3 to Sandymount
To see the tailor's other life.
Up the street a block ahead of me
He leans a little to the right, limping,
Twirling a latchkey on a chain.
Under one arm the *Independent* stains
The inseam of his summer jacket.
His shoes need new soles, a shine.
Then up three steps he pauses, latching the gate,
While at the path's far end a woman
Opens a sky-blue door, stepping into sunset
With the posture of a flower after a bright day.
He nods his head a little to the left
And passes by. She follows him inside.

I am early for the drink he offered me,
So instead of standing on the curb
I lean against the back wall of the tiny house
Beside an open window, waiting, I tell myself,
For them to look changed, wanting company.
Inside the tailor drops the *Independent*
On a chair. He drapes his summer coat
Across the shoulders of a dresser's dummy
And making a labored breathing noise
Collapses on the couch.
His wife brings in the mail.
He picks through it,

Probes bills and pushes it all away.
She wants to know what sale made his day.
He grunts. He rubs his knees,
His hands otherworldly in soft yellow light.
He moves them back and forth, snagging wool,
And tells her how he dressed me,
How I ought to be arriving any time.

   "You might have phoned me up," she says,
Jumping up and running out of the room.
I glance down at my sack in their flower bed
Then back at his hands. I wonder how he touches her.
I wonder what she does.
Pray that he doesn't? Brace herself?
Bend so that his hands may convalesce in her hair?
As if to answer me she comes back in and kneels,
Taking his left shoe in her hand.
She removes the shoe, a thinning sock,
And there before a slipper swallows it
A luxurious pink foot wiggles its toes.
The tailor's head reclines. His eyelids droop.
The fingers of one hand continue stroking
Slowly back and forth one woolen track,
Raising a private memory.
I will him to speak, but only an echo sounds—

    Hats are in,
    Hemlines fall,
    And we are easier to look at.

I don't feel easier to look at.
Ashamed, happy, I raise my sack of wool

And walk around to ring the bell.
Inside I ask the tailor's wife for a changing room.
I open up my sack. She looks inside and smiles.
"This way," she says.

   The small side room she leads me to
Is seldom used, severely dusted.
While changing I count thirty photographs
Of the tailor with men of every age.
In every frame, the two stand chatting in a yard,
The backyard, or warming their backsides at a fireplace.
I get a funny feeling along my neck,
Not that I feel fear or any threat.
At first I had thought Big Family,
But something told me No, not Family.

Finished now I step out in the hall
And meet his wife. I follow her,
And entering the room I nearly knock
The dresser's dummy to the floor.
I catch it just in time.
"Ever wonder how you learn that?"
A voice from the couch says.
"Somehow you do, and you remember."
I laugh. I say hello. I sit.
His wife jabs a poker among coals
Then settles a tray with whiskey and glasses between us.
They question me as we drink,
The tailor raised up on one elbow
His wife straight-backed, leaning a little forward in her chair.
They want to know about America,
About the way we dress and why.
They ask about Family. They measure me,
Asking about Government and Jobs

And how we treat the old.
He says he might retire;
He wonders if they'd find a life in Boston or New York.
I will not share hard news,
But I tell them to stay home.
The tailor, sitting up, refills my glass.
"To that," he says. Our glasses clink together.

When I turn to his wife she has a camera.
She orders us to stand before the mantel
Then focuses and shoots, settling my place
Among preserved encounters in their changing room.
Sitting down we work on drinks.
It is dark outside. And silent.
Over voices low we talk until dinner,
The tailor leaning sideways along the couch,
His eyes half-open, his fingers stroking wool.
My fingers copy his and I am getting it,
Peace that comes of stroking out the day,
The tailor with his mouthful of pins,
Indoors on the shopper's street
In summer's heavenly weather.

Demons & Lava

Guerrero hugs the foul line,
Guarding against the extra base,
The mental lapse in which the ball plays him.
So far, the breaks have gone his way.
In the home-half of the sixth
He drilled a hanging curve and 48,000 cheered
As he trotted toward the high fives of his mates.
That's where it stands—his team
Two runs up in the twilight innings.
✛
The fans in Kevin's bungalow can feel it,
Pressure on every pitch, the closing gap,
Heat that bullies Hollywood.
"We're sweating like bleacher bums,"
Bob says to Katie. "You should feel at home."
They smoke and swallow bourbon,
Leaning into the racket of the swamp-cooler
(The radio in there somewhere) to catch the play-by-play.

"The Braves," Bob says. "They're still on top by four."
Katie drains Manhattans from a shaker,
Reminding Kevin she's a White Sox fan.
"I want my friendship back," he says,
And laughs. Everybody takes it up.
Katie concedes that she can root for L.A., too,
Because the Sox are in the other league.
"You'll be converted," Charles says,
"Tomorrow night above Elysian Park. Wear blue."
"We're buddies until Series time," she says.

Charles fills between-innings gaps with a guitar
And "Hobo Bill" becomes their cutoff man
Between baseball and personal freight.
Kevin drinks to Charles and to Hollywood.
He drinks to the mercury dipping into the 90s,

To the dog that has puffed all night
As if he couldn't catch his breath,
Sleeping now with his snout in Katie's purse.
He drinks to his birthday coming up,
To the time they'll all be in their thirties.

"Time to make it or go belly-up," Katie says.
The dog turns thirty in his sleep,
Praying for relocation to a cooler climate.
The others pray for money.
Charles casts out over the phone,
Hoping to reel in tickets for tomorrow.
"Not for me," Bob says.
I'm out of here after midnight."

"Stop fidgeting," Katie says.
Mixing another round she winks at Bob,
Who labors in his head to grip the turning point
The evening's act of significance.
Was it only in the home-half of the sixth
When Pedro jerked one into the atmosphere?
"L.A. is giving us a lesson," Kevin says.
✝
Charles judo-chops the air,
Cutting Kevin off in mid-joke. Top of the ninth.
The first two batters swing and fall,
But #3 smashes a screamer up the line—
Pedro's moment. A nifty crossover step and lunge
Bring ball and glove together above the bag.
Then it occurs.
Pedro bobbles the ball. Pain disrupts his face.
The fans forget the tying run approaching the plate
Because their leading hitter is down,
Making like his leg is a bag of broken glass.
"Why was he still in the game?" Kevin says.

"Dumb," Bob says, "like staying in town too long."
"Lava," Charles says. "Demons and lava."

They look at each other and talk in lower voices.
In their minds, they're scrutinized through x-rays;
They're falling asleep for arthroscopic surgery.
"Maybe I've stayed too long," Bob says.
As a unit they recoil,
Confessing how much they want to stop smoking,
Questioning mysterious ailments, demons and lava,
Sinister aches surfacing after thirty.

Like victims of lava they freeze.
"Do you know what Pedro's thinking?" Charles says.
"He's thinking he came up cleanly with the ball,
That as he pivoted he saw it—
Lava erupting in the coach's box. And demons."
They feel ironed into the rut of August,
Pressed by also-rans, bypassed.
Katie slumps in her chair, missing a signal,
And imagines the sleeping dog erased in a rundown.
Bob imagines the screams of his favorite players,
The national anthem sticking in everyone's throat,
The organist silent, possessing no music
For what happens out on the field.
Kevin asks how many Dodgers are over thirty.
All of them struggle to keep it down—
Anxiety gloved in the Bitterness Hour,
The I-May-Never-See-You-Again Hour.
In their stadium of friendship baselines wiggle,
Curvaceous whips in the claws of demons.

    ✛

They know how it feels to be packing with nowhere to go
After their names have been scratched from the roster.
The midnight hour.
They shorten their swings to protect the plate,
Waiting for a pitch they can handle.
Charles switches the radio off,
Jiggling change and keys in his pocket.
Bob begins thinking of nothing but Barstow.
That's how they go:
One drives to the desert, one to the shore,
While two walk hand-in-hand to bed.

Like flashlights that tire and don't shine so good,
Oh, honey, we've done the best that we could. . . .
—Chas. Duncan